WATER IN THE WILDERNESS

WATER IN THE WILDERNESS

God's Provision for Our Every Need

T.D. Jakes

DESTINY IMAGE® PUBLISHERS, INC.

P.O. Box 310, Shippensburg, PA 17257-0310

"Speaking to the Purposes of God for this Generation and for the Generations to Come."

This book and all other Destiny Image, Revival Press, Mercy Place, Fresh Bread, Destiny Image Fiction, and Treasure House books are available at Christian bookstores and distributors worldwide.

For a U.S. bookstore nearest you, call:
1-800-722-6774.
For more information on foreign distributors, call:
717-532-3040.
Or reach us on the Internet: www.destinyimage.com.

ISBN 10: 0-7684-2645-6
ISBN 13: 978-0-7684-2645-8

Previously Published: Copyright © 1994 by T.D. Jakes.
Previous Published: ISBN 1-56229-432-6

For Worldwide Distribution, Printed in the U.S.A.

1 2 3 4 5 6 7 8 9 10 11 / 11 10 09 08

Table of Contents

Foreword

I cannot think of a greater living example of the consistent ability to draw on the anointing of the Lord. T.D. Jakes is man without equal. There is much we can all learn from his words, his spirit and his passion in delivering the word of the Lord. Just watching him is a wonder in itself. The Presence of the Lord flows so freely from him as he teaches. He is simple, clear and honest in his delivery. Sometimes urgent, sometimes gentle, but always accurate and penetrating. He is a man whose inner focus is on the Lord Himself. Even in his most emotional presentation, you can also see the rest and peace in his eyes. The Holy Spirit will always move freely through those who have no other desire than to give the word of the Lord to hungry people. And make no mistake about it, God has much to say to His people. He has much He wants to communicate to the world around us. There is much to learn from the Bishop's words, but also his method, his passion and his love of the Lord Jesus Himself.

I first met the Bishop at a small conference in the Pocono Mountains where he was ministering. That was just before he wrote *Woman, Thou Art Loosed*. We literally walked into each other that fateful afternoon in the basement area of the conference center where vendors were displaying their products. The moment I touched him I prophesied about a book churning in his heart. A few weeks later he called me and the rest, as they say, is history.

There are three criteria we use when determining the possibility of publishing a new author. We look at the person, his message, and his ministry. In the Bishop's case, all three were intricately wrapped with integrity, gentleness and truth. We are proud to offer this work to the world. He is a man who has allowed the Lord to mold him into a vessel He can use to change the lives of millions around the world. We are grateful to be a part of God's plan for the life of Bishop T.D. Jakes.

Don Nori, Publisher
Destiny Image Publishers

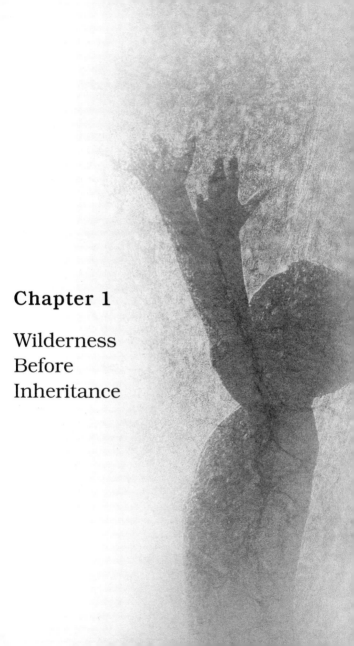

Chapter 1

Wilderness
Before
Inheritance

Wilderness Before Inheritance

*J*ehoram the son of Ahab began to reign over Israel in Samaria the eighteenth year of Jehoshaphat king of Judah, and reigned twelve years. And he wrought evil in the sight of the Lord; but not like his father, and like his mother: for he put away the image of Baal that his father had made. Nevertheless he cleaved unto the sins of Jeroboam the son of Nebat, which made Israel to sin; he departed not therefrom. And Mesha king of Moab was a *sheepmaster, and rendered unto the king of Israel an hundred thousand lambs, and an hundred thousand rams, with the wool. But it came to pass, when Ahab was dead, that the king of Moab rebelled against the king of Israel. And king Jehoram went out of Samaria the same time, and numbered all Israel. And he went and sent to Jehoshaphat the king of Judah, saying, The king of Moab hath rebelled against me: wilt thou go with me against Moab to battle? And he said, I will go up: I am as thou art, my people as thy people, and my horses as thy horses. And he said, Which way shall we go up? And he answered, The way through the wilderness of Edom* (2 Kings 3:1-8).

When you speak of the wilderness, your mind immediately imagines a dry place where nothing green grows. Everything in the wilderness is brown and unappealing to the eye. The environment of the wilderness is not brightened with any color. Everything in the wilderness has adapted itself to live in this type of climate. Rarely does it rain in the wilderness and when it does, plants store the moisture they need because there is no guarantee when it will rain again. When we are going through our wilderness experience, we must be like the trees and the other animals of the wilderness. We must learn to adapt our faith to the challenges a wilderness brings.

The animals in the wilderness have learned to travel and hunt at night because it is cooler at night. Spiritually, we too must learn to find a place where the Lord can minister to us in our wilderness. It is a place where He can give us instruction about what to do next. Like the trees that store up water, uncertain of when it will rain again, we must store up His Word in our hearts. Many of us are living in the wilderness for various reasons.

The wilderness is a place of dying, where all the things that cause you to stumble in your walk with God are killed. If you have ever watched a movie where people dared to enter the wilderness, with little or no understanding of life in the wilderness, they often did not survive there. Since they had no one to help or advise them, they tried to fight the elements in their own strength.

> *Finally you are in a place where I can speak to you.*

Likewise, many of us have been in the wilderness and we have tried unsuccessfully to fight the battle in our own strength. You see, the wilderness is a place where God says, "I finally have you in a place where I can speak to you." Because Jehoram was unprepared for life in the wilderness, he needed someone who knew something about the wilderness. Hence, he asked for Jehoshaphat's help.

Do not be fooled into thinking that you can ever be fully prepared for life in the wilderness. Sometimes, God leads us abruptly into the wilderness. He might have been trying to get you to come to Him or to get you to take your spiritual life more seriously. Perhaps He has been trying to draw your attention to the call He has placed in your life.

It is indeed a gamble that the Lord takes on us, for He knows that He cannot and will not override our will. But He also knows that it is truly our desire to do His will. Even the worst sinner is inwardly drawn to God even if he does not serve Him.

God loves you so much that He is willing to take just that type of risk on you. He knows that you may either serve Him or reject Him. You may say, "Lord, wherever You lead, I will follow, even through the wilderness." Or you may decide to say, "I can't deal with this. I thought life would be better than this. I quit."

But God knows that we must be tried in the fire so that we can become as pure as gold. God brings us into the wilderness to perfect our faith. You cannot have all pleasure without pain, neither can you enjoy only good times without adversity. Your faith is perfected in the furnace of affliction and adversity. There is something about going through dilemmas and crises that bring us to the place where we discover things about God which we would not have known under other circumstances.

> *Dilemmas and crises bring us closer to God.*

The sins in Jehoram's life prevented him from walking with God like he should have. His relationship with God was superficial. However, when he got in trouble he needed God as a fire escape. He called on God only when things were going bad. In essence, he wanted to use God as his servant, rather than serve God. He was interested in God only if God served his own selfish purpose.

Many of us have tried to use God for personal gain. We view God as a spiritual Santa Claus who is there at our every whim, one who will bring us gifts and presents that are beyond our reach. The only time we talk with Him is when we need something from Him.

> *Is God your spiritual Santa Claus?*

If a loved one becomes terminally ill, we immediately call on Him. We are ready to beat down the pastor's door so that he can pray for us, or we call on the saints and implore their spiritual prayer and support. But, for some, as soon as the problem is over, what happens? We slump right back into the backslidden state we were in before the problem jolted us to pray. That is why many of us are constantly in problems.

God is fully aware of the sad fact that should we have all our needs met, we will never seek Him with all our hearts. Like the children of Israel, we tend to become arrogant and prideful, and forget the fact that we must fully acknowledge God in times of prosperity as well as adversity.

Jehoram was pretty smart, and he knew something about God. Realizing that he did not have a sound relationship with the Lord, he courted the friendship of one who did. He said to Jehoshaphat, king of Judah, "I have got to go out to fight and I want you to fight with me."

Jehoshaphat replied, "If you are going to war, I will go with you. My people are your people. I'm going to assume the responsibility of getting you the victory and all my captains and all my warriors are at your disposal." The next question was how to go about it.

They had to seek the mind of God on the matter. One of the servants of the king of Israel told Jehoshaphat about Elisha who had the word of the Lord. Jehoshaphat, Jehoram, and the king of Edom therefore traveled to see Elisha, the prophet.

> *And Elisha said unto the King of Israel, What have I to do with thee? get thee to the prophets of thy father, and to the prophets of thy mother.... As the LORD of hosts liveth, before whom I stand, surely, were it not that I regard the*

presence of Jehoshaphat the king of Judah, I would not look toward thee, nor see thee (2 Kings 3:13,14).

Sometimes, we are so obsessed with our destination that we forget that we must go through various phases to get there. For example, when a woman is pregnant, it is apparent to all that she is carrying a baby. After the baby is born, all we see is a beautiful baby. We forget that there is a process of bringing that baby into the world—a process that is painful for both the mother and the child.

There is a process involved in birthing a baby.

For the mother, it is the process of pushing this new delicate life out of her body where it has lived snugly for nine long, peaceful months. For the baby, it is the process of being pushed into a place that it perceives to be unfriendly and cold, very different from the home it had occupied for nine months.

Just like the baby in its mother's womb, we may have to let go of something that has become part of us. We are always confessing that we want the perfect will of God for our lives, but we must not forget the fact that we must conquer the obstacles that stand in the way of our future success in which God's ultimate will is realized.

King Jehoshaphat asked the question, "How shall we go up against Moab to get victory?" The unexpected answer was, "You have to go through the wilderness of Edom to get the victory" (See 2 Kings 3:8).

My friend, if you want to get the victory, you must be willing to go through the wilderness. I want to reiterate this fact: it is not always easy to get the victory because it belongs to the other side of the wilderness. You must be willing to go through a little time of abasement, confusion, adversity, and even opposition before you arrive at your destination.

> *If you want victory,*
> *you must go through the*
> *wilderness.*

Many may think that it is unfair to go through this phase. But you see, it is the wilderness that weeds out the saints from the "aint's." It is the wilderness that weeds out people who really want to do something for God from people who just have a momentary, superficial, mundane relationship with Him. It is the wilderness that makes a hypocrite back up and say, "I can't take it anymore." The wilderness, God's killing field, will weed out all the impostors because they cannot survive the adversity of the wilderness. The wilderness weeds out the saints from the "ain'ts."

> *The wilderness weeds out the saints from the "ain'ts.*

I want to warn you that you will have to go through the wilderness to attain the will of God for your life. The wilderness teaches us to stand; it teaches us to cast our cares upon Him. It teaches us to rely and totally depend on Him for life support, because we know in due season we shall reap if we faint not.

Some of us cannot handle the smallest problems. We feel that the hardships placed on our path indicate that God either has forsaken us or is punishing us for some sin we have committed. The devil has successfully employed that lie to deter us from seeking the heavenly Father. Do not for a moment think that you can do it on your own. You will fail woefully.

Remember Joshua and Caleb. Had they tried to enter the Promise Land on their own strength or cognizance, they would have perished in the wilderness. Even when life in the wilderness became dull and unappealing, they did not stop seeking God neither did they cease to rely on His guidance. Like Joshua and Caleb, we must be persistent in faith even in the wilderness where problems are at their peak.

The greatest battle that we face while we are in the wilderness is the one between the new and the old man. The old man that God is trying to kill in the wilderness refuses to die. It wants to resurrect old hurts and old problems. But, as new creatures in Christ Jesus, we must put the old man to death. Despite the situations you are facing, you must constantly remind yourself that you are a new creature and the old man is *dead!*

> *Our greatest battle is between the new and the old man.*

Thoughts and Reflections

Chapter 2

Who Is
Your
God?

Who Is Your God?

Jesus answered and said, unto him....
It is written thou shalt worship the
Lord thy God, and him only shalt thou
serve (Luke 4:8b).

My God is the Alpha and the Omega, the Beginning and the End. There is nothing too hard for Him. There is nothing He cannot handle. Because we know who we are in Christ Jesus and what we mean to our heavenly Father, satan tries to discourage us. He tries to use sickness, financial problems, family stress, and anything and everything you can think of to incapacitate us. The question you must ask yourself is, ""Who is my God? Whom do I serve?" Then answer the question, "My God is the Way-Maker." The Bible says that if God be for us, who can be against us? (See Romans 8:31.)

God is so real in my inward man. He has not only washed away all my sins, but He has filled my cup with His love so that my cup bubbles over. He is the Lover of my soul; He is the Answer to my every need; He is my Burden-Bearer. Maybe you are the kind of person who can handle everything that comes your way, but I can't. However, I know someone who is able to take it. His name is Jesus Christ.

The enemy fights those who know who they are and whose they are. The Bible affirms that God is faithful (see 1 Cor. 1:9). The Word of God states, "But to us there is but one God, the Father, of whom are all things, and we in him; and one Lord Jesus Christ, by whom are all things, and we by him" (1 Cor. 8:6).

Are you aware that the more the enemy fights you, the greater the indication that blessings are on the way? You must be cognizant of this fact as a Christian. If you do not know that about life, you cannot make it. You have got to know that it is because you are on the verge of a miracle that the devil is fighting you. He is fighting you so hard because you are getting closer to your deliverance, and the closer you get, the greater the struggle.

> *The more the enemy fights you, the more blessings are on the way.*

If you hold out a little while longer, God's going to give you the victory in every circumstance of your life. I am learning to be encouraged when I meet with obstacles because I see them as an indication of a fresh move of God in my life.

When people ask you who your God is, how do you respond? With confidence, your shoulders held high, and a smile on your face you can say, "He is everything I will ever need. He is my Father, the Creator of Heaven and Earth, and the One who sustains the universe. He is Jehovah, the *I am that I am.*"

Thoughts and Reflections

_____

_____

_____

_____

_____

_____

_____

_____

_____

_____

_____

_____

_____

_____

_____

_____

_____

_____

_____

_____

_____

_____

_____

_____

_____

_____

_____

_____

_____

_____

_____

_____

_____

_____

_____

_____

_____

_____

_____

_____

_____

_____

_____

_____

_____

_____

Who Is Your God?

_____

_____

_____

_____

_____

_____

_____

_____

_____

_____

_____

_____

_____

_____

_____

_____

_____

_____

_____

_____

_____

_____

_____

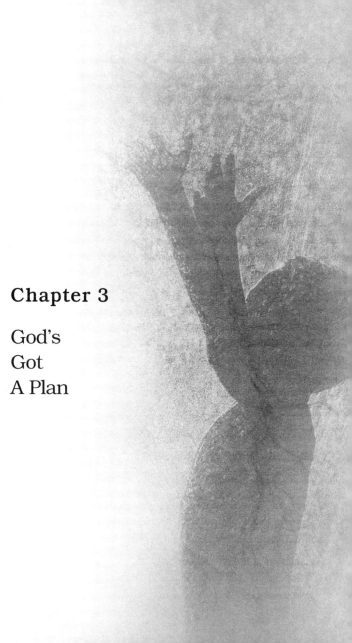

Chapter 3

God's
Got
A Plan

God's Got a Plan

When you are in the wilderness, you must find out what the plan of God is for you. You cannot rely on anyone else's plan. Only a plan from God will suffice in the wilderness.

God has not promised that you will not go through hardship, neither has He promised that you will not experience adversity. But listen to what He says: "When you pass through the waters, I will be with you. When you go through the flood, I'll be there. Should you have to go through fire, I will be there. As I was with Shadrach, Meshach, and Abednego, so will I be with you. I will be the fourth One in the furnace."

> *Only a plan from God will suffice in the wilderness.*

I am very grateful that the Lord's been walking with me all these years. I say this not because I have not been through anything, or that I have not faced various challenges and dark moments in life, but I do recognize that the Lord has been the fourth One in the fiery furnace. He has protected me from the scorching of the flames. When the pressure and the flames seemed as if they would engulf me, His words of assurance would comfort me.

There are many who would have lost their mind had the Lord not been on their side. They would have gone crazy and lost control, but the Lord comforted them in their darkest hour. It is not that we did not go through the wilderness but when we went through it, God was with us. God will be with you when mama, daddy, sister, and brother leave. When the folks you thought would be with you all the way, walk out of the door, God says, "Lo, I am with you always even unto the ends of the world."

You need not fear the wilderness if you take God with you everywhere you go. I must take Him with me everywhere I go, or else I would fall on my face. I truly need the Lord for I cannot function without Him. I need Him in the morning; I need Him in the noon day; I need Him when the sun is down. I need Him to run my business; I need Him to teach me how to be a good father; I need Him to be a good husband. Don't you try to be anything without God, because you will not succeed.

The enemy may come to discourage you. He may whisper to your mind that God will not help you or that you might have committed a horrible sin that has brought God's wrath on you. Satan thinks that he catches the Lord by surprise. But, oh, is he wrong! God is a God of plans. He is a God of order. As the God who knows all things, He is never surprised by the attack of the enemy. While the enemy is planning his strategies, God has already made a counter-plan for him. He has already made a way of escape for you. Yes, you must trust Him.

Trust Him.

Peter asked the Lord Jesus if he could join Him on the sea. After the Lord told him to come, Peter got out of the boat and walked on the sea until he took his eyes off of Jesus.

Maybe you are in trouble right now. Maybe you are reading this book, trying to find answers to your situation. Maybe you have been trying to run your life without God or you have been trying to deal with your wilderness without God's help. You may be convinced you know what you are doing and that you are not obligated to listen to anyone. Be careful, for pride comes before a fall. My friend, you do need God. You need Him to help you to hold your mind together.

You need Him when you are at the breaking point and people have disappointed you. Nobody else but God will get up with you at 3:00 a.m. and hold you in His arms. Nobody else but God can comfort you when you are depressed.

Only God can supernaturally soothe your nerves and quell your worries. Only He can

44

give you that peace that passes all under-standing. When the Scripture talks about the peace that passes all understanding, it refers to a peace that is anointed. When peo-ple look at your situation, and then look at you, they will be confused. They will say, "Why is he so peaceful? Doesn't he realize that he has nothing? Everything he had is gone. Why is he so peaceful?" It is simply the God-given peace that you enjoy. Try it. Believe me; you will like it. God says, "It's going to be all right. Just trust Me, just lean on Me, and look to Me for total deliverance."

His peace is
anointed peace.

You might not be able to see how it will work out, but you've got to trust that before it is all over, God's going to give you the vic-tory. You see, God's got a plan!

Thoughts and Reflections

_____

_____

_____

_____

_____

_____

_____

_____

_____

_____

_____

_____

_____

_____

_____

_____

_____

_____

_____

_____

_____

_____

_____

_____

_____

_____

_____

_____

_____

_____

_____

_____

_____

_____

_____

_____

_____

_____

_____

_____

_____

_____

_____

_____

Chapter 4

The
Power
of Praise

The Power of Praise

I will bless the Lord at all times: his praise shall continually be in my mouth. My soul shall make her boast in the Lord: the humble shall hear thereof, and be glad. O magnify the Lord with me, and let us exalt his name together. I sought the Lord, and he heard me, and delivered me from all my fears. They looked unto him, and were lightened: and their faces were not ashamed (Psalms 34:1-5).

Praise is magnifying and exalting the Lord in our hearts. Praise is glorifying the

Lord with the fruit of our lips. When we begin to praise God with all our heart, we lose sight of the magnitude of our problems as we gain a vision of the greatness of our Lord.

In order to truly praise God, we must learn to go beyond ourselves and our human limitations. Many times when the enemies of Israel encamped around them, God told Joshua to send out the tribe of Judah first. Judah means praise. Judah marched before the enemies of Israel, armed with nothing but instruments of praise.

When the tribe of Judah began to praise God with their whole heart, God set ambushes among the enemy and confused them. The same principle happens in the spirit realm. When we really begin to praise God, our praise confounds the enemy, and demonic forces begin to withdraw their power and influence.

> *Our praise confounds the enemy.*

For though we walk in the flesh we do not war after the flesh: (For the weapons of our warfare are not carnal, but mighty through God to the pulling down of strongholds;) Casting down imaginations, and every high thing that exalteth itself against the knowledge of God, and bringing into captivity every thought to the obedience of Christ (2 Corinthians 10:3-5).

Praise and worship is the most profound way of expressing our love to the Father. God loves to be praised and worshiped. However, in order to praise God, we must understand the power that praise and worship wield. Praise and worship can break demonic strongholds that have bound us.

Praise and the Word of God are able to pull down strongholds. There is power in praise and worship. Let us pause here to examine this concept of praise as a weapon against spiritual strongholds.

First, let us define strongholds. Strongholds are roadblocks or stumbling blocks that prevent God's people from truly releasing themselves in praise and worship to God. There are many strongholds, but we will only talk about a couple of them.

The erection of strongholds take place in our thought process.

Strongholds take place in our thought process.

For example, suppose you were visiting a new church where their method of praise and worship is somewhat different from yours. Immediately, your mind tells you that their way is wrong, or, worse still, that they are not saved. This is a stronghold. Remember that a stronghold is a belief system that is contrary to what God's Word says. You see, in this case, your church has spoken against being too expressive in worship and praise. To them praise and worship does not have to be loud and noisy.

I have noticed that many people in the church do not know how to worship or praise the Father. We get nervous when someone during service gets too loud and starts to worship God differently from our normal style. We want to worship God in low voices, and that's only on Sunday mornings in our lofty buildings. We must appear "respectable." But in the clubs, or at baseball and football games, the same people will yell and make as much noise as they can without getting the least bit nervous or losing their "respectability."

The Lord loves to hear us praise His holy name and doesn't get nervous when we either become too loud or too quiet. It is we who discriminate about how to praise God. We must be very cautious about this area of our lives. If we allow satan to build up strongholds, we create more roadblocks in our minds that prevent us from praising God freely. Someone once said, "A free person is a dangerous person because he does not allow anyone to dictate what he says or does except the Lord!"

> *The Lord loves to hear us praise Him.*

Once the believers understand how satan uses strongholds to keep them from releasing themselves in praise and worship, they are better prepared to use their weapons of praise and worship. Someone once said, "We must understand that the area of thought is both the first and final battlefield. It begins with the mind before it goes to any other area."

Hence, satan fights us in our minds to such great extent.

What is Praise?

Praise is replacing your thoughts and the enemy's thoughts with the thoughts of God. The Word of God, the Name of Jesus, and the Blood of Jesus are weapons of God that transform and change our thoughts. Although many people may not realize this truth, a tremendous amount of power is released when praise is offered to God. All too often we take this weapon for granted. Imagine what David felt as he composed his psalms. When you take God's thoughts and enter into praise, you become like a battering ram against the strongholds that satan has erected in your mind.

Praise replaces your thoughts with thoughts of God.

Another stronghold that we must pull down is the idea that the believer should look sad and gloomy whenever he is going through a difficult time. We think that the devil is having his heyday with us, using us like a dust rag. This ought not to be. We must speak God's Word over the state of our emotions. It is indeed possible to change the state of your mind through the Word of God. Satan tries to destroy you through your mind. Allow the Lord to direct you.

> *Speak God's Word over your emotions.*

Have you ever heard the voice of God through the thick of the night and thereby you get your victory? It wasn't because you were smart; it wasn't because you were taught; it wasn't because you were so good, but it came just because you learned to say, "Lord, I love You, I praise You. I'm in trouble, but I still love You. I have trials, but I still love You. I don't feel well this morning, but I still love You. I have bills I can't pay, but I still love You." David said, "I will bless the Lord at all times."

Music and Praise

But now bring me a minstrel. And it came to pass, when the minstrel played, that the hand of the Lord came upon him (2 Kings 3:15).

In this Scripture, Elisha requested a musician because he saw the need for music. We too need some music in the church. Music can change attitudes and emotions within us. It has the ability to mold and shape thoughts. We have an assortment of instruments—drums, tambourines, organs, and pianos. One king obtained the victory just because he had an orchestra with him. The musicians of the temple of the Lord played musical instruments until the enemy of Israel became confused and started killing one another.

God loves music. He said, "If you want Me to move, play Me some music. Get Me somebody who has an instrument." When Saul was possessed with demons, David played his harp until the demons left Saul. There is something about the anointed music of the Holy Spirit.

Anointed music will drive out demons, trouble, and sickness. That is why you must be very careful about the type of music that you allow to enter your soul for it has a great effect on your inner man (spirit man). Get some anointed and powerful music. If you want your body to be healed, get some music that speaks healing into your body. Elisha said, "Get me somebody who will play me a song." The Bible says that when the minstrel began to play, the Word of the Lord began to flow out of Elisha's mouth.

Don't you allow anyone to take your song from your lips. You may lose friends, but don't lose your song. You might not sing well in the hearing of other people, but keep your song. You might croak like a frog, but keep your song. David said, "Make a joyful noise unto God, all ye lands" (Psalm 66:1). Paul demonstrated that if you have a song, you can sing your way out of the jail. If you have a song, you can encourage yourself. Even when there is nobody around to encourage you, and you feel all alone, if you have a song you can encourage yourself in the Lord.

God will move when you start praising Him. When you start to praise God, He will come in the middle of your drought, in the middle of your wilderness, and in the middle of your dry place, and say, "I've got a plan!"

> *God will move when you*
> *praise Him.*

Thoughts and Reflections

The Power of Praise

_____

_____

_____

_____

_____

_____

_____

_____

_____

_____

_____

_____

_____

_____

_____

_____

_____

_____

_____

_____

_____

_____

_____

_____

_____

_____

_____

_____

_____

_____

_____

_____

_____

_____

_____

_____

_____

_____

_____

_____

_____

_____

_____

_____

_____

_____

_____

_____

_____

_____

_____

_____

_____

_____

_____

_____

_____

_____

_____

_____

_____

_____

_____

_____

_____

_____

_____

Chapter 5

Intimacy
in Worship

Intimacy in Worship

*Thou shalt worship the Lord thy God,
and him only shalt thou serve* (Matthew
4:10).

Whatever we worship is what we ultimately will end up serving. Our nature de-
mands that we worship something. What we
worship is up to us.

*But the hour cometh, and now is,
when the true worshippers shall worship the Father in spirit and in truth:
for the Father seeketh such to worship
him* (John 4:23).

To experience true worship you must first develop a relationship with the Father. All relationships are dependent upon good communication. For us as believers, prayer is the means of communicating with the Father. This relationship can be likened to that of a man and his wife. There is the sense of intimacy, closeness, and oneness. It is the closeness that you should never share with anyone else.

When a man and a woman first get married, their relationship is new and exists on that level of looking deeply into each other's eyes. This is the honeymoon stage. At this stage, each worships the ground that the other walks on. Their focus is on each other. But, as time goes on, the honey dries a little and the moon begins to lose its luster. The newness in their relationship begins to wear off, giving way to a different dimension in their relationship.

> *This is the honeymoon state.*

They begin to know each other on a more intimate level. They can feel each other's hurts and desires. They avoid what will hurt or jeopardize their closeness. They don't hide anything, rather, they express their feelings in confidence and trust. They trust each other with their weaknesses and shortcomings, confident that they will not be used against them. This is the kind of desire that the Lord wants us to enjoy with Him, a close relationship that leads to intimate worship.

There are different kinds of gods we may find ourselves bowing to. Some of us worship our children. Some worship money. Some worship sin. Some worship themselves while others worship all types of things: a paycheck, reputation, etc.

Have you ever observed a Christian who recently got saved? He worships God with a deep gratitude for his salvation. The first stage in the romance of a man and woman is often referred to as infatuation. This is also typical of the first stage of our relationship with Christ. The dictionary describes *infatuation* as "to behave foolishly, to inspire with foolish and unreasoning love or attachment." However, as we mature in the Lord, this type of attraction takes on a new and higher dimension. Infatuation, like romance, operates more on feelings than reality, on the external than on the internal. It is more fleeting than stable, more inconsistent than constant. But mature love is consistent because it is based on commitment. Commitment (covenant) is what sustains any lasting and stable relationship.

> *Commitment sustains relationships.*

When a man first falls in love with a woman, it might have been her beauty and figure that attracted him. But after the marriage, when he wakes up in the morning to bad breath, hair rollers, or a body that has birthed two or three children, infatuation goes out the window. It is neither infatuation nor romance that keeps him coming home, but the commitment to the vow that he made at the altar that sustains the relationship.

The same commitment must define our relationship with the Lord. We must graduate from the point where we praise and worship God only for what He does for us. We must praise Him for who He is. Our worship must transcend a superficial expression that is dependent on our feelings alone. We must develop a relationship that is consistent even in the midst of trials. The trials should deepen our relationship with the Lord, not weaken it.

Wilderness experiences will mature our relationship with the Lord to the degree that our worship is expressed not only externally by the fruit of our lips in praise, but also our love for Him expressed through our continual obedience. It is the obedience that flows from the heart, freely without coercion.

Thoughts and Reflections

_____

_____

_____

_____

_____

_____

_____

_____

_____

_____

_____

_____

_____

_____

_____

_____

_____

_____

_____

_____

_____

_____

_____

_____

_____

_____

_____

_____

_____

_____

_____

_____

_____

_____

_____

_____

_____

_____

_____

_____

_____

_____

_____

_____

_____

_____

_____

_____

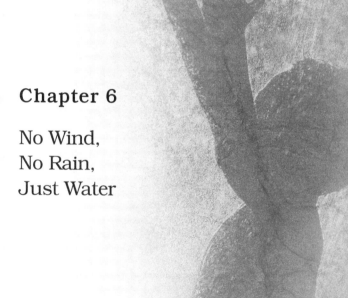

Chapter 6

No Wind,
No Rain,
Just Water

No Wind, No Rain, Just Water

For thus saith the Lord, Ye shall not
see wind, neither shall ye see rainryet
that valley shall be filled with water
(2 Kings 3:17).

Can you still believe this promise after
all you have been through - after suffering
and being deprived of winds and rain? God
said He is going to give you the water. Since
the king of Moab did not see rain, he appar-
ently did not expect to see water. And when
he came upon the mountain top, and looked
down in the valley, the rays of the sun on

the water gave the appearance of blood. He thought it was the blood of his enemies.

He ran down there to kill them, but what he thought was blood was just water.

Some of you should have been dead and long gone, but God saw your blood and sent you the water. You could have died of spiritual dehydration, but He did not send wind or rain, just water. You could have given up, but you did not give up. I could have passed out, but I am not out. There is water in my family, water in my relationships, water in my church, water in my preaching, water in my business, water in my home, water in my career, water, water, water, water...water everywhere.

There are some people in the wilderness who don't have any water yet, and unless they have someone to minister to them as Elisha ministered to Jehoshaphat and Jehoram, they will die in the wilderness without water. Someone must preach the gospel until their dry areas are made wet. You don't have to give up, you don't have to give in, you don't have to quit. God said He will fill those dry areas of your life with water.

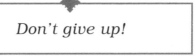

Don't give up!

If you have been going though dry places and wilderness for a long time, God is saying, "Dig some ditches, because I'm getting ready to bless you and your latter day is going to be greater than your former day." God will fill the ditches in your homes and marriages with water. To the ditches of finances, God says, "I will fill them with water." To the ditches of your emotions, He says, "Get your mind ready, get your attitude right, get your heart fixed, because when I open up the windows of heaven I am going to pour you out a blessing that you will not have room enough to receive."

It is a blessing that will be pressed down, shaken together, and running over. Are you ready for the blessing? Some people may be thinking of quitting, but don't quit. The moment that you are ready to throw in the towel, when you think you cannot take it any more, it is then that God will send you His blessing. Do not allow Satan to discourage you and thus deprive you of God's blessing. The devil is a liar and the father of lies.

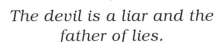

The devil is a liar and the father of lies.

God repeats, "Dig ditches in your valley. Get ready! You have been suffering for a long time, but I am getting ready to bless you. I want you to dig ditches and get ready. As soon as you are ready, the answer will be there." When the answer comes, it is going to come in the spirit and not in the flesh. Once the ditches have been dug, there will be no warning or sign, no clouds, no winds, not even rain, just water.

In the natural when it is about to rain, one can tell by the wind and the clouds, but God is saying, "I'm going to send you a blessing that has no sign, and it will not have any warning. Everything may be stagnant, but I am going to move in the midst of your stagnation. Just because you do not see any wind does not mean that I am not getting ready to bless you. Get ready!"

You might look up and not see any sign in the climate. Maybe you do not see the clouds forming in the sky. I know you are use to lightning, but there might not be any. I know that you are use to thunder before the outpouring, but you may not hear the thunder. There might not be wind. It might not even rain, but just because there is no wind, nor rain, does not mean that there won't be water.

84

You must know that God is going to bless you. I don't care if the wind is not blowing or the thunder is not sounding, you must know that God cannot lie. If He has promised to bless you, then He will bless you. If He has promised to deliver you, then He will deliver you. If He has promised to bring you out, then He is able. The Lord is more than able. No wind, no rain, but there will still be blessing without warning. You must expect the blessing to come.

When God was ready to send the flood, He did not just send water down on Noah. The Bible says that He broke up the cisterns of the deep, and water started coming up out of the ground (Gen. 7:11). Yes, water started coming out of the dry places.

Do you have any dry places? God is saying that is where the water is going to come from. Have you had struggles in any areas of your life? God says that is where the water is going to come from. Do you have frustrations? God says He is going to send the water out of your pain and agony.

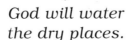

*God will water
the dry places.*

Maybe the water is trickling at first. Have you ever said, "I'm getting something, but that is not enough. I am better than what I used to be, but I still don't have that breakthrough. I am not saying that you are not blessing me, Lord, but something is missing out of my blessings. I am getting a little moisture?" But God is telling you now to wait on Him. You must learn how to wait. It is they that wait upon the Lord whose strength God will renew.

The Word of God says to wait. Wait even when it seems that nothing is happening. Wait while you are in the midst of the wilderness, when there is no sign of water. Wait on the perfect timing of God. Remember that He has a plan. He has not forsaken you even though the devil might have given you the impression that He has. As you wait, the Lord says, "Mount up with wings like eagles, run and don't be weary, walk and don't faint because that little drip of water is turning into a trickle, and the trickle will turn into a stream, and the stream will turn into a creek, the creek is going to turn into a lake, and the lake is going to turn into a river. And out of your belly, as the Word says, will flow rivers of living water" (John 7:38). "...will flow rivers of living water."

God will send you some water that will come out of your wilderness, and when it comes, it will be more than enough. If you do not have wind, do not worry. If you do not see rain, do not be perturbed. God is still going to give you the water. If you want the outpouring of God's Spirit, wait for Him. God will send you water in your dry places. God will send the water right into your personal wilderness.

Thoughts and Reflections

No Wind, No Rain, Just Water

_____
_____
_____
_____
_____
_____
_____
_____
_____
_____
_____
_____
_____
_____
_____
_____
_____
_____
_____
_____
_____
_____
_____
_____
_____

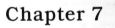

Chapter 7

Water
In the
Wilderness

Water in the Wilderness

And all the congregation of the children of Israel journeyed from the wilderness of Sin, after their journeys, according to the commandment of the Lord, and pitched in Rephidim: and there was no water for the people to drink.... And the people thirsted for water; and the people murmured against Moses, and said, Wherefore is this that thou hast brought us up out of Egypt, to kill us and our children and our cattle with thirst?...And the Lord said unto Moses, Go on before the people, and take with thee of the elders of Israel; and thy rod, wherewith thou smotest the river, take in thine hand, and go. Behold, I will stand before thee there upon the rock in Horeb; and thou shall smite the rock, and there shall come water out of it, that the people may drink. And Moses did so in the sight of the elders of Israel (Exodus 17:1,3,5,6).

There is water in the wilderness. If you are going through the dry places, is it not wonderful to know that God is a cool drink while in a hot and thirsty land? When you run out of water, run out of friends, run out of ideas, and run out of plans, God says, "You are going through a tough time, but do not worry; I have a plan."

> *Don't worry*
> *—God has a plan.*

God has a way of escape. I do not know what wilderness you are going through, but I do know this much about God: He will step into the middle of the wilderness of your dilemma. He is not confined to the church building. He is also God in your wilderness.

He will come into your house. He will come on your job. He will take care of you. Have you ever found yourself praising God in the car, and the praise reaches a height where tears well up in your eyes, and you know you must stop the car for fear that you might hit someone? Have you been in a situation where you are worshiping God, and people around you thought that you were talking to yourself?

Has the Lord ever visited you in an awkward place, such as the bus stop or a subway, where you really do not have the freedom to praise God? However, the praise got so high within you that it took every muscle of your will power to keep quiet.

I enjoy being by myself with God. If I shout too loud in public, and the people get nervous, I cannot be very free. But when I am alone, I can call on God as loud as I want, and I can cry as long and as loud as I want to cry. If I want to tap my foot, I can tap my foot. If I feel like moaning, I can lie down and moan without the fear that someone is commenting about it. When I wave my hands, He understands.

You may be in a dry place where there is no water. Or you may be in the wilderness or in a deep valley, but remember, God provides water in the dry places.

> *God provides*
> *refreshing water.*

When I was in Arizona last year on a preaching tour, I had a chance to see a dry riverbed. As I walked down into the dry riverbed, I sensed in my spirit that the Lord was ministering to me. Once there was water in the riverbed, but now it had gone dry. Yet, you could tell that there used to be water there, but due to the dryness in the atmosphere, it had dried up. It is amazing that the sun was able to evaporate that much water. The rocks could still be seen at the bottom of the riverbed. Yet no life existed there.

Unfortunately, this is the way some churches are today. There once was water in these churches. There used to be some glory in their midst. The church used to be spiritually alive, but now there is no sign of life.

A principle needs to be underscored here. If the river dried up over here, then you must go over there. If you are going through a dry time in your life, then you must find water. If you do not find some water, you will be like those animals that died without water.

I am conscious of the fact that I need some water every hour of the day. I am not in need of someone who would beat me over the head with the Word just to make me feel bad, but I do need someone who can tell me that I can make it. I need someone to tell me that God is my deliverer, that He is my Joy in the midst of sorrow, that He is my Healer, the One Who makes a way where there seems to be none.

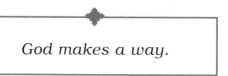

God makes a way.

I need someone to tell me He is a strong Tower, that He is the Doctor in the sick room, the Lawyer in the courtroom, and the Water in the wilderness. God says, "This is what I want you to do while you are still down in the dry riverbed: dig ditches in your valley." Now it may have been enough for God to fill your riverbed, but God says He is going to bless you much more than the riverbed can contain.

God says, "You had better begin to dig those ditches in the riverbed, because what you need is not deep enough for My supply, and when I do bless you, My blessing is going to be so much greater than your present capacity to receive. So dig some ditches for the outpouring. Contrary to how bleak and distraught the situation may be or how devastating the trial or crisis, remember My promise: I will provide water in the wilderness.

Thoughts and Reflections

_____

_____

_____

_____

_____

_____

_____

_____

_____

_____

_____

_____

_____

_____

_____

_____

_____

_____

_____

_____

_____

_____

_____

_____

_____

_____

_____

_____

_____

_____

_____

_____

_____

_____

_____

_____

_____

_____

_____

_____

_____

_____

_____

_____

_____

_____

_____

_____

_____

_____

_____

_____

_____

_____

_____

_____

_____

_____

_____

_____

_____

_____

_____

_____

_____

_____

_____

_____

_____

Bonus Material

Chapter 1

Woman, Thou
Art Loosed!

Infirmed Woman

A *nd, behold, there was a woman*
which had a spirit of infirmity eight-
een years, and was bowed together, and
could in no wise lift up herself. And when
Jesus saw her, He called her to Him, and
said unto her, Woman, thou art loosed
from thine infirmity (Luke 13:11-12).

The Holy Spirit periodically lets us catch a
glimpse of the personal testimony of one of the
patients of the Divine Physician Himself. This
woman's dilemma is her own, but perhaps you
will find some point of relativity between her
case history and your own. She could be like

someone you know or have known; she could even be like you.

There are three major characters in this story. These characters are the person, the problem and the prescription. It is important to remember that for every person, there will be a problem. Even more importantly, for every problem, our God has a prescription!

Jesus' opening statement to the problem in this woman's life is not a recommendation for counseling—it is a challenging command! Often much more is involved in maintaining deliverance than just discussing past trauma. Jesus did not counsel what should have been commanded. I am not, however, against seeking the counsel of godly men. On the contrary, the Scriptures say:

> *Blessed is the man that walketh not in the counsel of the ungodly, nor standeth in the way of sinners, nor sitteth in the seat of the scornful* (Psalm 1:1).

> *Where no counsel is, the people fall: but in the multitude of counsellors there is safety* (Proverbs 11:14).

What I want to make clear is that after you have analyzed the condition—after you have understood its origin—it will still take the authority of God's Word to put the past under your feet!

This woman was suffering as a result of something that attacked her 18 years earlier. I wonder if you can relate to the long-range after-effects of past pain? This kind of trauma is as fresh to the victim today as it was the day it occurred. Although the problem may be rooted in the past, the prescription is a present word from God! The Word is the same yesterday, today and forevermore! (See Hebrews 13:8.) That is to say, the word you are hearing today is able to heal your yesterday!

> *His word will heal*
> *your yesterday.*

Jesus said, "Woman, thou art loosed." He did not call her by name. He wasn't speaking to her just as a person. He spoke to her femininity. He spoke to the song in her. He spoke to the lace in her. Like a crumbling rose, Jesus spoke to what she could, and would, have been. I believe the Lord spoke to the twinkle that existed in her eye when she was a child; to the girlish glow that makeup can never seem to recapture. He spoke to her God-given uniqueness. He spoke to her gender.

Her problem didn't begin suddenly. It had existed in her life for 18 years. We are looking at a woman who had a personal war going on inside her. These struggles must have tainted many other areas of her life. The infirmity that attacked her life was physical. However, many women also wrestle with infirmities in emotional traumas. These infirmities can be just as challenging as a physical affliction. An emotional handicap can create dependency on many different levels. Relationships can become crutches. The infirmed woman then places such weight on people that it stresses a healthy relationship. Many times such emotional handicaps will spawn a series of unhealthy relationships.

> *For thou hast had five husbands; and he whom thou now hast is not thy husband: in that saidst thou truly* (John 4:18).

Healing cannot come to a desperate person rummaging through other people's lives. One of the first things that a hurting person needs to do is break the habit of using other people as a narcotic to numb the dull aching of an inner void. The more you medicate the symptoms, the less chance you have of allowing God to heal you.The other destructive tendency that can exist with any abuse is the person must keep increasing the dosage. Avoid addictive, obsessive relationships.

Avoid addictive, obsessive relationships.

If you are becoming increasingly dependent upon anything other than God to create a sense of wholeness in your life, then you are abusing your relationships.

Clinging to people is far different from loving them. It is not so much a statement of your love for them as it is a crying out of your need for them. Like lust, it is intensely selfish. It is taking and not giving. Love is giving. God is love. God proved His love not by His need of us, but by His giving to us.

> *For God so loved the world, that He gave His only begotten Son, that whosoever believeth in Him should not perish, but have everlasting life* (John 3:16).

The Scriptures plainly show that this infirmed woman had tried to lift herself. People who stand on the outside can easily criticize and assume that the infirmed woman lacks effort and fortitude. That is not always the case. Some situations in which we can find ourselves defy will power. We feel unable to change. The Scriptures say that she "could in no wise lift up herself." That implies she had employed various means of self-ministry. Isn't it amazing how the same people who lift up countless others, often cannot lift themselves?

This type of person may be a tower of faith and prayer for others, but impotent when it comes to her own limitations. That person may be the one others rely upon. Sometimes we esteem others more important than ourselves. We always become the martyr. It is wonderful to be self-sacrificing, but watch out for self-disdain! If we don't apply some of the medicine that we use on others to strengthen ourselves, our patients will be healed and we will be dying.

I shall not die, but live, and declare the works of the Lord (Psalm 118:17).

Many things can engender disappointment and depression. In this woman's case, a spirit of infirmity had gripped her life. A spirit can manifest itself in many forms. For some it may be low self-esteem caused by child abuse, rape, wife abuse or divorce. I realize that these are natural problems, but they are rooted in spiritual ailments. One of the many damaging things that can affect us today is divorce, particularly among women, who often look forward to a happy relationship. Little girls grow up playing with Barbie and Ken dolls, dressing doll babies and playing house. Young girls lie in bed reading romance novels, while little boys play ball and ride bicycles in the park.

Jesus heals broken hearts.

Whenever a woman is indoctrinated to think success is romance and then experiences the trauma of a failed relationship, she comes to a painful awakening. Divorce is not merely separating; it is the tearing apart of what was once joined together. Whenever something is torn, it does not heal easily. But Jesus can heal a broken or torn heart!

> *The Spirit of the Lord is upon Me, because He hath anointed Me to preach the gospel to the poor; He hath sent Me to heal the brokenhearted, to preach deliverance to the captives, and recovering of sight to the blind, to set at liberty them that are bruised* (Luke 4:18).

Approximately five out of ten marriages end in divorce. Those broken homes leave a trail of broken dreams, people, and children. Only the Master can heal these victims in the times in which we live. He can treat the long-term effects of this tragedy. One of the great healing balms of the Holy Spirit is forgiveness. To forgive is to break the link between you and your past. Sadly enough, many times the person hardest to forgive is the one in the mirror. Although they rage loudly about others, people secretly blame themselves for a failed relationship. Regardless of who you hold responsible, there is no healing in blame! When you begin to realize that your past does not necessarily dictate the outcome of your future, then you can release the hurt. It is impossible to inhale new air until you exhale the old. I pray that as you continue reading, God would give the grace of releasing where you have been so you can receive what God has for you now. Exhale, then inhale; there is more for you.

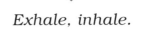

Exhale, inhale.

Perhaps one of the more serious indictments against our civilization is our flagrant disregard for the welfare of our children. Child abuse, regardless of whether it is physical, sexual or emotional, is a terrible issue for an innocent mind to wrestle with. It is horrifying to think that little children who survive the peril of the streets, the public schools and the aggravated society in which we live, come home to be abused in what should be a haven. Recent statistics suggest that three in five young girls in this country have been or will be sexually assaulted. If that many are reported, I shudder to think of those that never are reported but are covered with a shroud of secrecy.

If by chance you are a pastor, please realize that these figures are actually faces in your choir, committees, etc. They reflect a growing amount of our congregational needs. Although this book focuses on women, many men also have been abused as children. I fear that God will judge us for our blatant disregard of this need in our messages, ministries, and prayers. I even would suggest that our silence contributes to the shame and secrecy that satan attaches to these victimized persons.

Whenever I think on these issues, I am reminded of what my mother used to say. I was forever coming home with a scratch or cut from schoolyard play. My mother would take the band-aid off, clean the wound and say, "Things that are covered don't heal well." Mother was right. Things that are covered do not heal well.

Perhaps Jesus was thinking on this order when He called the infirmed woman to come forward. It takes a lot of courage even in church today to receive ministry in sensitive areas. The Lord, though, is the kind of physician who can pour on the healing oil. Uncover your wounds in His presence and allow Him to gently heal the injuries. One woman found healing in the hem of His garment (Mark 5:25-29). There is a balm in Gilead! (Jer. 8:22).

Even when the victim survives, there is still a casualty. It is the death of trust. Surely you realize that little girls tend to be trusting and unsuspicious. When those who should nurture and protect them violate that trust through illicit behavior, multiple scars result. It is like programming a computer with false information; you can get out of it only what has been programmed into it.

When a man tells a little girl that his perverted acts are normal, she has no reason not to believe that what she is being taught is true. She is devoted to him, allowing him to fondle her or further misappropriate his actions toward her. Usually the abuser is someone very close, with access to the child at vulnerable times. Fear is also a factor, as many children lay down with the cold taste of fear in their mouths. They believe he could and would kill them for divulging his liberties against them. Some, as the victims of rape, feel physically powerless to wrestle with the assailant.

What kind of emotions might this kind of conduct bring out in the later life of this person? I am glad you asked. It would be easy for this kind of little girl to grow into a young lady who has difficulty trusting anyone! Maybe she learns to deal with the pain inside by getting attention in illicit ways. Drug rehabilitation centers and prisons are full of adults who were abused children needing attention.

Not every abused child takes such drastic steps. Often their period of behavioral disorder dissipates with time. However, the abused child struggles with her own self-worth. She reasons, "How can I be valuable if the only way I could please my own father was to have sex with him?" This kind of childhood can affect how later relationships progress. Intimidated by intimacy, she struggles with trusting anyone. Insecurity and jealousy may be constant companions to this lady, who can't seem to grasp the idea that someone could love her.

> *Your childhood affects relationships.*

There are a variety of reactions as varied as there are individuals. Some avoid people who really care, being attracted to those who do not treat them well. Relating to abuse, they seem to sabotage good relationships and struggle for years in worthless ones. Still others may be emotionally incapacitated to the degree that they need endless affirmation and affection just to maintain the courage to face ordinary days.

The pastor may tell this lady that God is her heavenly Father. That doesn't help, because the problem is her point of reference. We frame our references around our own experiences. If those experiences are distorted, our ability to comprehend spiritual truths can be off center. I know that may sound very negative for someone who is in that circumstance. What do you do when you have been poorly programmed by life's events? I've got good news! You can re-program your mind through the Word of God.

> *Reprogram your mind with the Word of God!*

Do not conform any longer to the pattern of this world, but be transformed by the renewing of your mind. Then you will be able to test and approve what God's will is—His good, pleasing and perfect will (Romans 12:2 NIV)

The Greek word *metamorphôo* is translated as "transformed" in this text. Literally, it means to change into another form! You can have a complete metamorphosis through the Word of God. It has been my experience as a pastor who does extensive counseling in my own ministry and abroad, that many abused people, women in particular, tend to flock to legalistic churches who see God primarily as a disciplinarian. Many times the concept of fatherhood for them is a harsh code of ethics. This type of domineering ministry may appeal to those who are performance-oriented. I understand that morality is important in Christianity; however, there is a great deal of difference between morality and legalism. It is important that God not be misrepresented. He is a balanced God, not an extremist.

> *God is balanced*
> *—not extreme.*

The Word became flesh and made His dwelling among us. We have seen His glory, the glory of the One and Only, who came from the Father, full of grace and truth (John 1:14 NIV).

The glory of God is manifested only when there is a balance between grace and truth. Religion doesn't transform. Legalism doesn't transform. For the person who feels dirty, harsh rules could create a sense of self-righteousness. God doesn't have to punish you to heal you. Jesus has already prayed for you.

Sanctify them through Thy truth: Thy word is truth (John 17:17).

Jesus simply shared grace and truth with that hurting woman. He said, "Woman, thou art loosed." Believe the Word of God and be free. Jesus our Lord was a great emancipator of the oppressed. It does not matter whether someone has been oppressed socially, sexually or racially; our Lord is an eliminator of distinctions.

> *The Lord eliminates distinctions.*

There is neither Jew nor Greek [racial], there is neither bond nor free [social], there is neither male nor female [sexual]: for ye are all one in Christ Jesus (Galatians 3:28).

I feel it is important to point out that this verse deals with unity and equality in regard to the covenant of salvation. That is to say, God is no respecter of persons. He tears down barriers that would promote prejudice and separation in the Body of Christ. Yet it is important also to note that while there is no distinction in the manner in which we receive any of those groups, there should be an appreciation for the uniqueness of the groups' individuality. There is a racial, social and sexual uniqueness that we should not only accept, but also appreciate. It is cultural rape to teach other cultures or races that the only way to worship God is the way another race or culture does. Unity should not come at the expense of uniqueness of expression. We should also tolerate variance in social classes. It is wonderful to teach prosperity as long as it is understood that the Church is not an elite organization for spiritual yuppies only— one that excludes other social classes.

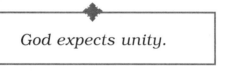

God expects unity.

If uniqueness is to be appreciated racially and socially, it is certainly to be appreciated sexually. Male and female are one in Christ. Yet they are unique and that uniqueness is not to be tampered with. Let the male be masculine and the female be feminine! It is a sin for a man to misrepresent himself by conducting himself as a woman. I am not merely speaking of homosexuality. I am also talking about men who are feminine in their mannerisms. Many of these men may not be homosexual in their behavior, but the Bible says that they must be healed of feminine mannerisms, or vice versa. It is equally sad to see a masculine woman. Nevertheless, God wants them healed, not hated!

Know ye not that the unrighteous shall not inherit the kingdom of God? Be not deceived: neither fornicators, nor idolaters, nor adulterers, nor effeminate, nor abusers of themselves with mankind....
(1 Corinthians 6:9).

I realize that these behavioral disorders are areas that require healing and prayer. My point is simply that unity does not negate uniqueness. God is saying, "I don't want men to lose their masculine uniqueness." This is true racially, socially, and sexually. God can appreciate our differences and still create unity. It is like a conductor who can orchestrate extremely different instruments into producing a harmonious, unified sound. Together we produce a sound of harmony that expresses the multifaceted character of God.

Having established the uniqueness of unity, let us now discuss some aspects of the uniqueness of the woman. By nature a woman is a receiver. She is not physically designed to be a giver. Her sexual and emotional fulfillment becomes somewhat dependent on the giving of her male counterpart (in regard to intimate relationships). There is a certain vulnerability that is a part of being a receiver. In regard to reproduction (sexual relationships), the man is the contributing factor, and the woman is the receiver.

What is true of the natural is true of the spiritual. Men tend to act out of what they perceive to be facts, while women tend to react out of their emotions. If your actions and moods are not a reaction to the probing of the Holy Spirit, then you are reacting to the subtle taunting of the enemy. He is trying to produce his destructive fruit in your home, heart, and even in your relationships. Receiver, be careful what you receive! Moods and attitudes that satan would offer, you need to resist. Tell the enemy, "This is not me, and I don't receive it." It is his job to offer it and your job to resist it. If you do your job, all will go well.

> *Be careful of what*
> *you receive!*

Submit yourselves, then, to God. Resist the devil, and he will flee from you (James 4:7 NIV).

Don't allow the enemy to plug into you and violate you through his subtle seductions. He is a giver and he is looking for a receiver. You must discern his influence if you are going to rebuke him. Anything that comes, any mood that is not in agreement with God's Word, is satan trying to plug into the earthly realm through your life. He wants you to believe you cannot change. He loves prisons and chains! Statements like, "This is just the way I am," or "I am in a terrible mood today," come from lips that accept what they ought to reject. Never allow yourself to settle for anything less than the attitude God wants you to have in your heart. Don't let satan have your day, your husband, or your home. Eve could have put the devil out!

Neither give place to the devil (Eph.4:27).

It is not enough to reject the enemy's plan. You must nurture the Word of the Lord. You need to draw the promise of God and the vision for the future to your breast. It is a natural law that anything not fed will die. Whatever you have drawn to the breast is what is growing in your life. Breastfeeding holds several advantages for what you feed: (a) It hears your heartbeat; (b) it is warmed by your closeness; (c) it draws nourishment from you. Caution: Be sure you are nurturing what you want to grow and starving what you want to die.

As you read this, you may feel that life is passing you by. You often experience success in one area and gross defeat in others. You need a burning desire for the future, the kind of desire that overcomes past fear and inhibitions. You will remain chained to your past and all the secrets therein until you decide: Enough is enough! I am telling you that when your desire for the future peaks, you can break out of prison. I challenge you to sit down and write 30 things you would like to do with your life and scratch them off, one by one, as you accomplish them. There is no way you can plan for the future and dwell in the past at the same time. I feel an earthquake coming into your prison! It is midnight—the turning point of days! It is your time for a change. Praise God and escape out of the dungeons of your past.

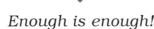

Enough is enough!

And at midnight Paul and Silas prayed, and sang praises unto God: and the prisoners heard them. And suddenly there was a great earthquake, so that the foundations of the prison were shaken: and immediately all the doors were opened, and every one's bands were loosed (Acts 16:25-26).

Have you ever noticed how hard it is to communicate with people who will not give you their attention? Pain will not continue to rehearse itself in the life of a preoccupied, distracted person. Distracted people almost seem weird. They do not respond! Every woman has something she wishes she could forget. There is a principle to learn here. Forgetting isn't a memory lapse; it is a memory release! Like carbon dioxide the body can no longer use, exhale it and let it go out of your spirit.

> *Brethren, I count not myself to have apprehended: but this one thing I do, forgetting those things which are behind, and reaching forth unto those things which are before, I press toward the mark for the prize of the high calling of God in Christ Jesus. Let us therefore, as many as be perfect, be thus minded: and if in any thing ye be otherwise minded, God shall reveal even this unto you* (Philippians 3:13-15).

Jesus set the infirmed woman free. She was able to stand upright. The crippling condition of her infirmity was removed by the God who cares, sees and calls the infirmity to the dispensary of healing and deliverance. You can call upon Him even in the middle of the night. Like a 24-hour medical center, you can reach Him at anytime. He is touched by the feeling of your infirmity.

> *For we have not an high priest which cannot be touched with the feeling of*

our infirmities; but was in all points tempted like as we are, yet without sin (Hebrews 4:15).

In the name of our High Priest, Jesus Christ, I curse the infirmity that has bowed the backs of God's women. I pray that, as we share together out of the Word of God, the Holy Spirit would roll you into the recovery room where you can fully realize that the trauma is over. I am excited to say that God never loosed anybody that He wasn't going to use mightily. May God reveal healing and purpose as we continue to seek Him.

Thoughts and Reflections

Infirmed Woman

_____

_____

_____

_____

_____

_____

_____

_____

_____

_____

_____

_____

_____

_____

_____

_____

_____

_____

_____

_____

_____

_____

_____

_____

◆

Bonus Material

Chapter 1

Can You Stand
to Be Blessed?

The Transformers

*B*ut as many as received Him, to them gave He power to become the sons of God, even to them that believe on His name (John 1:12).

I pray that we as Christians never lose our conviction that God does change lives. We must protect this message. Our God enables us to make the radical changes necessary for fulfilling our purposes and responsibilities. Like the caterpillar that eats and sleeps its way into change, the process occurs gradually, but nonetheless powerfully. Many people who will rock this world are sleeping in the cocoon of obscurity, waiting for their change to come. The Scriptures declare, "…it is high time to awake out of sleep: for now is our salvation nearer than when we believed" (Rom. 13:11).

A memory of my twin sons playing on the floor when they were children tailors the continuity of this text for me. They were playing with a truck, contributing all the sounds of grinding gears and roaring engines. I didn't pay much attention as I began unwinding from the day's stresses and challenges. Distractedly, I glanced down at the floor and noticed that the boys were now running an airplane down an imaginary runway. I asked, "What happened to the truck you were playing with?" They explained, "Daddy, this is a transformer!" I then inquired, "What is a transformer?" Their answer brought me into the Presence of the Lord. They said, "It can be transformed from what it was before into whatever we want it to be!"

Suddenly I realized that God had made the first transformer! He created man from dust. He created him in such a way that, if need be, He could pull a woman out of him without ever having to reach back into the dust. Out of one creative act God transformed the man into a marriage. Then He transformed the marriage into a family, the family into a society, etc. God never had to reach into the ground again because the power to transform was intrinsically placed into man. All types of potential were locked into our spirits before birth. For the Christian, transformation at its optimum is the outworking of the internal. God placed certain things in us that must come out. We house the prophetic power of God. Every word of our personal prophetic destiny is inside us. He has ordained us to be!

> *Before I formed thee in the belly I knew thee; and before thou camest forth out of the womb I sanctified thee, and I ordained thee a prophet unto the nations* (Jeremiah 1:5).

Only when we are weary from trying to unlock our own resources do we come to the Lord, receive Him, and allow Him to release in us the power to become whatever we need to be. Actually, isn't that what we want to know: our purpose? Then we can use the power to become who we really are. Life has chiseled many of us into mere fragments of who we were meant to be. To all who receive Him, Christ gives the power to slip out of who they were forced into being so they can transform into the individual they each were created to be.

Salvation as it relates to destiny is the God-given power to become what God has eternally decreed you were before. "Before what?" you ask; before the foundation of the world. What Christians so often refer to as grace truly is God's divine enablement to accomplish predestined purpose. When the Lord says to Paul, "My grace is sufficient for thee..." (2 Cor. 12:9), He is simply stating that His power is not intimidated by your circumstances. You are empowered by God to reach and accomplish goals that transcend human limitations! It is important that each and every vessel God uses realize that they were able to accomplish what others could not only because God gave them the grace to do so. Problems are not really problems to a person who has the grace to serve in a particular area.

How many times have people walked up to me and said, "I don't see how you can stand this or that." If God has given us the grace to operate in a certain situation, those things do not affect us as they would someone else who does not have the grace to function in that area. Therefore, it is important that we not imitate other people. Assuming that we may be equally talented, we still may not be equally graced. Remember, God always empowers whomever He employs. Ultimately, we must realize that the excellency of our gifts are of God and not of us.

He doesn't need nearly as much of our contributions as we think He does. So it is God who works out the internal destinies of men. He gives us the power to become who we are eternally and internally.

> *Wherefore, my beloved, as ye have always obeyed, not as in my presence only, but now much more in my absence, work out your own salvation with fear and trembling. For it is God which worketh in you both to will and to do of His good pleasure* (Philippians 2:12-13).

Today in the Body of Christ a great deal of emphasis is placed on the process of mentoring. The concept of mentoring is both scriptural and effective; however, as we often do, many of us have gone to extremes. Instead of teaching young men to pursue God, the ultimate Rabbi, they are running amuck looking for a man to pour into them. All men are not mentored as Joshua was—under the firm hand of a strong leader. Some, like Moses, are prepared by the workings of the manifold wisdom of God. This latter group receives mentoring through the carefully orchestrated circumstances that God ordains to accomplish an end result. Regardless of which describes your ascent to greatness, it is still God who "worketh in you both to will and to do." When you understand this, you appreciate the men or the methods God used, but ultimately praise the God whose masterful ability to conduct has crescendoed in the finished product of a man or woman of God.

> *And the Lord said unto Moses, Gather unto Me seventy men of the elders of Israel, whom thou knowest to be the elders of the people, and officers over them; and bring them unto the tabernacle of the congregation, that they may stand there with thee* (Numbers 11:16).

In keeping with this mentoring concept, let's consider Moses' instructions when asked to consecrate elders in Israel. I found it interesting that God told Moses to gather unto Him men whom he knew were elders. God says, "I want you to separate men to be elders who are elders." You can only ordain a man to be what he already is. The insight we need to succeed is the discernment of who is among us. Woe unto the man who is placed into what he is not. Moses was to bring these men into a full circle. In other words, they were to be led into what they already were. Perhaps this will further clarify my point: When the prodigal son was in the "hog pen," it was said, "And when he came to himself..." (Luke 15:17). We are fulfilled only when we are led into being who we were predestined to be. Real success is coming to ourselves.

The thing that gives a man power to arise above his circumstances is his coming to himself. You feel fulfilled when you achieve a sense of belonging through your job, family, or ministry. Have you ever met anyone who left you with a feeling of familiarity-almost as if you had known the person? A sense of bonding comes out of similarities. Likewise, there are certain jobs or ministries that feel comfortable, even if they are tasks you have never done before. If you are discerning, you can feel a sense of belonging in certain situations. However, weary are the legs of a traveler who cannot find his way home. Spiritual wanderings plague the lives of many people who wrestle with discontentment. May God grant you success in finding your way to a sense of wholeness and completion.

Change is a gift from God. It is given to the person who finds himself too far removed from what he feels destiny has ordained for him. There is nothing wrong with being wrong-but there is something wrong with not making the necessary adjustments to get things right! Even within the Christian community, some do not believe in God's ability to change the human heart. This unbelief in God's ability to change causes people to judge others on the basis of their past. Dead issues are periodically revived in the mouths of gossips. Still, the Lord progressively regenerates the mind of His children. Don't assume that real change occurs without struggle and prayer. However, change can be achieved.

God exalted Him to His own right hand as Prince and Savior that He might give repentance and forgiveness of sins to Israel (Acts 5:31 NIV). The Bible calls change repentance. Repentance is God's gift to a struggling heart who wants to find himself. The Lord wants to bring you to a place of safety and shelter. Without the Holy Spirit's help you can search and search and still not find repentance. The Lord will show the place of repentance only to those who hunger and thirst after righteousness. One moment with the Spirit of God can lead you into a place of renewal that, on your own, you would not find or enjoy. I believe it was this kind of grace that made John Newton record, "It was grace that taught my heart to fear and grace my fears relieved. How precious did that grace appear the hour I first believed" (Amazing Grace, early American melody). When God gives you the grace to make changes that you know you couldn't do with your own strength, it becomes precious to you.

For ye know how that afterward, when he would have inherited the blessing, he was rejected: for he found no place of repentance, though he sought it carefully with tears (Hebrews 12:17). Brother Esau sought for the place of repentance and could not secure it. To be transformed is to be changed. If you are not moving into your divine purpose, you desperately need to repent. "Repent" has a strong negative connotation for the person indoctrinated to be-lieve that repentance is a fearful and dangerous action. It is not dangerous. Repentance is the prerequisite of revival. There cannot be revival without prayerful repentance. John the Baptist taught Israel, "Repent ye: for the kingdom of heaven is at hand" (Matt. 3:2). If God wants you to change, it is because He wants you to be prepared for what He desires to do next in your life. Get ready; the best is yet to come.

For whom He did foreknow, He also did predestinate to be conformed to the image of His Son, that He might be the firstborn among many brethren (Romans 8:29).

And be not conformed to this world: but be ye transformed by the renewing of your mind, that ye may prove what is that good, and acceptable, and perfect, will of God (Romans 12:2).

Now let's deal with some real issues! The word *conformed* in Romans 8:29 is summormorphoo (Strong's #4832)[1], which means "to be fashioned like or shaped into the image or the picture" of—in this case—Christ. God has predestined you to shape up into a picture of Christ in the earth. Christ is the firstborn of a huge family of siblings who all bear a striking resemblance to their Father. The shaping of a will, however, requires a visit to the Garden of Gethsemane. *Gethsemane* literally means oil press (Strong's #1068)[2]. God presses the oil of His anointing out of your life through adversity. When you forsake your will in order to be shaped into a clearer picture of Christ, you will see little drops of oil coming out in your walk and work for God. In short, He predestined the pressing in your life that produces the oil. As you are pressed, you gradually conform to the image of your predestined purpose.

In Romans 12:2 we are instructed not to be conformed to this world. Literally, it says we are not to be conformed to the same pattern of this world. The text warns us against submitting to the dictates of the world. We are to avoid using those standards as a pattern for our progress. On a deeper level God is saying, "Do not use the same pattern of the world to measure success or to establish character and values." The term *world* in Greek is aion (Strong's #165)[3], which refers to ages. Together these words tell us, "Do not allow the pattern of the times you are in to become the pattern that shapes your inward person."

At this point I can almost hear someone saying, "How do you respond to the preexisting circumstances and conditions that have greatly affected you?" Or, "I am already shaped into something less than what God would want me to be because of the times in which I live or the circumstances in which I grew up." I am glad you asked these things. You see, every aspect of your being that has already been conformed to this age must be transformed! The prefix *trans-* implies movement, as in the words transport, translate, transact, transition, etc. In this light, transform would imply moving the form. On a deeper level it means moving from one form into another, as in the tadpole that is transformed into the frog, and the caterpillar into the butterfly. No matter what has disfigured you, in God is the power to be transformed.

Many individuals in the Body of Christ are persevering without progressing. They wrestle with areas that have been conformed to the world instead of transformed. This is particularly true of us Pentecostals who often emphasize the gifts of the Spirit and exciting services.

It is imperative that, while we keep our mode of expression, we understand that transformation doesn't come from inspiration! Many times preachers sit down after ministering a very inspiring sermon feeling that they accomplished more than they actually did. Transformation takes place in the mind.

The Bible teaches that we are to be renewed by the transforming of our minds (see Rom. 12:2; Eph. 4:23). Only the Holy Spirit knows how to renew the mind. The struggle we have inside us is with our self-perception. Generally our perception of ourselves is affected by those around us. Our early opinion of ourselves is deeply affected by the opinions of the authoritative figures in our formative years. If our parents tend to neglect or ignore us, it tears at our self-worth. Eventually, though, we mature to the degree where we can walk in the light of our own self-image, without it being diluted by the contributions of others.

When we experience the new birth, we again go back to the formative years of being deeply impressionable. It's important to be discerning in who we allow to influence us in the early years. Whenever we become intimate with someone, the first thing we should want to know is, "Who do you say that I am?" Our basic need is to be understood by the inner circle of people with whom we walk. However, we must be ready to abort negative, destructive information that doesn't bring us into an accelerated awareness of inner realities and strengths. Jesus was able to ask Peter, "Who do you say that I am?" because He already knew the answer! (See Matthew 16:15). To ask someone to define you without first knowing the answer within yourself is dangerous. When we ask that kind of question, without an inner awareness, we open the door for manipulation. In short, Jesus knew who He was.

The Lord wants to help you realize who you are and what you are graced to do. When you understand that He is the only One who really knows you, then you pursue Him with fierceness and determination. Pursue Him! Listen to what Paul shares at the meeting on Mars Hill.

And hath made of one blood all nations of men for to dwell on all the face of the earth, and hath determined the times before appointed, and the bounds of their habitation; that they should seek the Lord, if haply they might feel after Him, and find Him, though He be not far from every one of us: for in Him we live, and move, and have our being; as certain also of your own poets have said, For we are also His offspring (Acts 17:26-28).

The basic message of this passage is that God has set the bounds on our habitations. He knows who we are and how we are to attain. This knowledge, locked up in the counsel of God's omniscience, is the basis of our pursuit, and it is the release of that knowledge that brings immediate transformation. He knows the hope or the goal of our calling. He is not far removed from us; He reveals Himself to people who seek Him. The finders are the seekers. The door is opened only to the knockers and the gifts are given to the askers! (See Luke 11:9.) Initiation is our responsibility. Whosoever hungers and thirsts shall be filled. Remember, in every crisis He is never far from the seeker!

Transforming truths are brought forth through the birth canal of our diligence in seeking His face. It is while you are in His presence that He utters omniscient insights into your individual purpose and course. Jesus told a woman who had been wrestling with a crippling condition for 18 years that she was not really bound-that in fact she was loosed! Immediately she was transformed by the renewing of her mind. (See Luke 13:11-13.) It is no wonder David said, "In Thy presence is fulness of joy" (Ps. 16:11b). The answer is in the Presence-the Presence of God, not man! There is a renewing word that will change your mind about your circumstance. Just when the enemy thinks he has you, transform before his very eyes!

No matter who left his impression upon you, God's Word prevails! The obstacles of past scars can be overcome by present truths. Your deliverance will not start in your circumstances; it will always evolve out of your mentality. As the Word of God waxes greater, the will of men becomes weaker. Paul said in Ephesians 5:26 that Jesus cleanses by the "washing of water by the word." So turn the faucet on high and ease your mind down into the sudsy warm water of profound truth. Gently wash away every limitation and residue of past obstacles and gradually, luxuriously, transform into the refreshed, renewed person you were created to become. Whenever someone tells you what you can't do or be, or what you can't get or attain, then tell them, "I can do all things through Christ who strengthens me! I am a transformer!"

Thoughts and Reflections

CAN YOU STAND TO BE BLESSED?

Bonus Material

Chapter 1

Naked and
Not Ashamed

The Fear of the Father

Have you ever tasted that cold, acid-like taste of fear? I mean the kind of fear that feels like a cinder block is being dragged across the pit of your stomach. It's the kind where cold chills trimmed with a prickly sensation flood your body, adorning itself in a distinct sense of nausea. No matter how strong we are, there is always something that can cause the heart to flutter and the pulse to weaken.

Fear is as lethal to us as paralysis of the brain. It makes our thoughts become arthritic and our memory sluggish. It is the kind of feeling that can make a graceful person stumble up the stairs in a crowd. You know what I mean—the thing that makes the articulate stutter and the rhythmic become spastic. Like an oversized growth, fear soon becomes impossible to camouflage. Telltale signs like trembling knees or quivering lips betray fear even in the most disciplined person. Fear is the nightmare of the stage; it haunts the hearts of the timid as well as of the intimidated.

From the football field to the ski slope, fear has a visa or entrance that allows it to access the most discriminating crowd. It is not prejudiced, nor is it socially conscious. It can attack the impoverished or the aristocratic. When it grips the heart of a preacher, his notes turn into a foreign language and his breathing becomes asthmatic.

To me, there is no fear like the fear of the innocent. This is the fear of a child who walks into a dark basement to find the light switch far from reach—and every mop and bucket becomes a sinister, sleazy creature whose cold breath lurks upon the neck of life's little apprentice. I can remember moments as a child when I thought my heart had turned into an African tom-tom that was being beaten by an insane musician whose determined beating would soon break through my chest like the bursting of a flood-engorged dam.

Even now I can only speculate how long it took for fear to give way to normalcy, or for the distant rumble of a racing heart to recede into the steadiness of practical thinking and rationality. I can't estimate time because fear traps time and holds it hostage in a prison of icy anxiety. Eventually, though, like the thawing of icicles on the roof of an aged and sagging house, my heart would gradually melt into a steady and less pronounced beat.

I confess that maturity has chased away many of the ghosts and goblins of my youthful closet of fear. Nevertheless, there are still those occasional moments when reason gives way to the fanciful imagination of the fearful little boy in me, who peeks his head out of my now fully developed frame like a turtle sticks his head out of its shell with caution and precision.

The Love of the Father

My little children, of whom I travail in birth again until Christ be formed in you (Galatians 4:19).

Thank God that He understands the hidden part within each of us. He understands the child in us, and He speaks to our blanket-clutching, thumb-sucking infantile need. In spite of our growth, income, education, or notoriety, He still speaks to the childhood issues of the aging heart. This is the ministry that only a Father can give.

Have you ever noticed that you are never a grown-up to the ones who birthed you? They completely disregard the gray hairs, crowfeet, and bulging, blossoming waistlines of abundant life. No matter how many children call you "Dad" or "Mom," to your parents you are still just a child yourself. They seem to think you have slipped into the closet to put on grown-up clothes and are really just playing a game. They must believe that somewhere beneath the receding hairline there is still a child, hiding in the darkness of adulthood. The worst part about it is (keep this quiet), I think they are right!

The Lord looks beyond our facade and sees the trembling places in our lives. He knows our innermost needs. No matter how spiritually mature we try to appear, He is still aware that lurking in the shadows is a discarded candy wrapper from the childish desire we just prayed off last night—the lingering evidence of some little temper or temptation that only the Father can see hiding within His supposedly "all grown-up" little child.

It is He alone whom we must trust to see the very worst in us, yet still think the very best of us. It is simply the love of a Father. It is the unfailing love of a Father whose son should have been old enough to receive his inheritance without acting like a child, without wandering off into failure and stumbling down the mine shaft of lasciviousness. Nevertheless, the Father's love throws a party for the prodigal and prepares a feast for the foolish. Comprehend with childhood faith the love of the Father we have in God!

When the disciples asked Jesus to teach them to pray, the first thing He taught them was to acknowledge the *fatherhood* of God. When we say "Our Father," we acknowledge His fatherhood and declare our sonship. Sonship is the basis for our relationship with Him as it relates to the privilege of belonging to His divine family. Similarly, one of the first words most babies say is "Daddy." So knowing your father helps you understand your own identity as a son or daughter. Greater still is the need to know not only *who* my father is, but *how he feels about me.*

It is not good to deny a child the right to feel his father's love. In divorce cases, some women use the children to punish their ex-husbands. Because of her broken covenant with the child's father, the mother may deny him the right to see his child. This is not good for the child! Every child is curious about his father.

Philip saith unto Him, Lord, show us the Father, and it sufficeth us (John 14:8).

Philip didn't know who the Father was, but he longed to see Him. I can still remember what it was like to fall asleep watching television and have my father pick up my listless, sleep-ridden frame from the couch and carry me up the stairs to bed. I would wake up to the faint smell of his "Old Spice" cologne and feel his strong arms around me, carrying me as if I weighed nothing at all. I never felt as safe and protected as I did in the arms of my father—that is, until he died and I was forced to seek refuge in the arms of my heavenly Father.

What a relief to learn that God can carry the load even better than my natural father could, and that He will never leave me nor forsake me! Perhaps it was this holy refuge that inspired the hymnist to pen the hymn, "What a fellowship, what a joy divine. Leaning on the everlasting arms" (from the lyrics of "Leaning on the Everlasting Arms," Elisha A. Hoffman, 1887).

Fear or Respect?

> *And unto man He said, Behold, the fear of the Lord, that is wisdom; and to depart from evil is understanding* (Job 28:28).

The Hebrew term for *"fear"* in this verse is *yir'ah*, according to *Strong's Exhaustive Concordance of the Bible.* It means a moral fear, or reverence. So what attitude should we have toward our heavenly Father? The Bible declares that we should have a strong degree of reverence for Him. But a distinction must be made here: There is a great deal of difference between fear and reverence.

The term *reverence* means to respect or revere; but the term *fear* carries with it a certain connotation of terror and intimidation. That kind of fear is not a healthy attitude for a child of God to have about his heavenly Father. The term rendered "fear" in Job 28:28 could be better translated as "respect." Fear will drive man away from God like it drove Adam to hide in the bushes at the sound of the voice of his only Deliverer. Adam said, "I heard Thy voice in the garden, and I was afraid..." (Gen. 3:10). That is not the reaction a loving father wants from his children. I don't want my children to scatter and hide like mice when I approach! I may not always agree with what they have done, but I will always love who they are.

I remember an occasion when some students from the elementary school my sons attended saw me for the first time. Because I stand a good 6'2" and weigh over 250 pounds, the little children were completely astonished. The other children told my sons, "Look at how big your dad is! I bet he would just about kill you. Aren't you afraid of him?" My sons quickly responded with glee, "Afraid of him? Nah, he's not mean. He's our dad!" They were not afraid of my stature because they were secure in our relationship. Does that mean they have never been punished? Of course not! What it does mean is they have never been abused! My love holds my judgment in balance.

As imperfect as I admit I am, if I know how to love my children, what about God? Oh friend, He may not approve of your conduct, but He still loves you! In fact, when you come to understand this fact, it will help you improve your conduct.

> *Or despisest thou the riches of His good-*
> *ness and forbearance and longsuffering;*
> *not knowing that the goodness of God*
> *leadeth thee to repentance?* (Romans 2:4)

If this text is true (and it is), then we must tell of God's goodness to those who need to repent. I believe the Church has confused *conviction* with *condemnation*. The Holy Spirit convicts us of sin. *Conviction* leads us to a place of deliverance and change. *Condemnation* leads us to the gallows of despair and hopelessness.

Why have we withheld from so many bleeding hearts the good news of the gospel? We have replaced this good news with the rambunctious ramblings of self-righteous rhetoric! I believe that we must assume the ministry of reconciliation and cause men to be reconciled back to their God.... We must remember that the only antidote is in the presence of the Lord....

Thoughts and Reflections

_____

_____

_____

_____

_____

_____

_____

_____

_____

_____

_____

_____

_____

_____

_____

_____

_____

_____

_____

_____

_____

_____

_____

Other Books, Videos, and Audiocassettes
by T.D. Jakes

Water in the Wilderness: God's Provision for Your Every Need

Just before you apprehend your greatest conquest, expect the greatest struggle. Many are perplexed who encounter this season of adversity. This book will show you how to survive the worst of times with the greatest of ease and will cause fountains of living water to spring out of the parched, sun-drenched areas in your life. This word is a refreshing stream in the desert for the weary traveler.

Why? Because You Are Anointed

Why do the righteous, who have committed their entire lives to obeying God, seem to endure so much pain and experience such conflict? These perplexing questions have plagued and bewildered Christians for ages. In this anointed and inspirational new book, Bishop T.D. Jakes, the preacher with the velvet touch and explosive delivery, provocatively and skillfully answers these questions and many more as well as answering the "Why" of the anointed.

Why? Workbook

Why? Workbook will help you to understand and overcome the difficulties that surround your own life. Over 150 thought-provoking questions will help you discover answers to the "whys" in your own life. Designed with a user-friendly, cutting-edge study system and answer key, it is an exciting and powerful tool for individual group studies.

Woman, Thou Art Loosed!

This book offers healing to hurting single mothers, insecure women, and battered wives.

Abused girls and women in crises are exchanging their despair for hope! Hurting women around the nation and those who minister to them are devouring the compassionate truths in Bishop T.D. Jakes' *Woman, Thou Art Loosed!* Also available as a workbook.

Can You Stand to Be Blessed?

Does any runner enter a race without training for it? Does a farmer expect a harvest without preparing a field? Do Christians believe they can hit the mark without taking aim? In this book T.D. Jakes teaches you how to unlock the inner strength to go on in God. These practical scriptural principles will release you to fulfill your intended purpose. The only question that remains is, *Can You Stand to Be Blessed?*

Manpower—Healing the Wounded Man Within (Audio Series)

Wounded men will experience the transforming power of God's Word in Manpower. satan has plotted to destroy the male, but God will literally raise up thousands of men through this life-changing, soul-cleansing, and mind renewing word. This four-part audio series is for every man who ever had an issue he could not discuss; for every man who needed to bare his heart and had no one to hear it.

Get in the Birth Position—Inducing Your God-Inspired Dreams

God's Word is steadfast. Nothing can stop what God has promised from coming to pass. However, you need to get ready. In this message T.D. Jakes shares the steps necessary to bring to birth the promises of God in your life.

The 25th Hour—When God Stops Time For You! (Video)

Have you ever thought, "Lord, I need more time?" Joshua thought the same thing, and he called upon the sun and moon to stand still! This message from Joshua 10 testifies of the mightiness of our God, who can stop time and allow His children to accomplish His purposes and realize the victory!

The Puppet Master

The vastness of God, His omnipotence and omnipresence, His working in the spirit world—these are concepts difficult to grasp. In this anointed message, T.D. Jakes declares God's ability to work for your deliverance, for He can go where you cannot go, do what you cannot do, and reach what you cannot reach!

Tell the Devil "I Changed My Mind!"

The Scriptures declare that it is with the mind that we serve the Lord. If there was ever a battleground that satan wants to seize and dominate in your life, it's right in the arsenals of your own mind. We must get the victory in our thought-life.

I believe that even now God is calling every prodigal son back home. Both the lost and the lukewarm are being covered and clothed with His righteousness and grace. I pray that this life-changing, soul-cleansing, mind-renewing message will help you find your way from the pit back to the palace.

He Loved Me Enough to Be Late
—Delayed But Not Denied

Many of us have wondered, "God, what is taking You so long?" Often God doesn't do what we think He will, when we think He will, because He loves us. His love is willing to be criticized to accomplish its purpose. Jesus chose to wait until Lazarus had been dead for several days, and still raised him up! This message will challenge you to roll away your doubt and receive your miracle from the tomb!

Out of the Darkness Into the Light

When Jesus healed a blind man on the Sabbath by putting mud on his eyes and telling him to wash, He broke tradition in favor of deliverance. The Church must follow this example. Are we willing to move with God beyond some of the things we have come from? Can we look beyond our personal dark moments to God? The Light of the world is ready to burst into our lives!

When Shepherds Bleed

Shepherding is a dangerous profession, and no one knows that better than a pastor. Drawing from personal encounters with actual shepherds in Israel and years of ministry, Bishop T.D. Jakes and Stanley Miller provide unique insight into the hazards faced by pastors today. With amazing perception, the authors pull back the bandages and uncover the open, bleeding wounds common among those shepherding God's flock. Using the skills of spiritual surgeons, they precisely cut to the heart of the problem and tenderly apply the cure. You'll be moved to tears as your healing process begins. Open your heart and let God lead you beside the still waters where He can restore your soul.

The Harvest

Have you been sidetracked by satan? Are you preoccupied with the things of this world? Are you distracted by one crisis after another? You need to get your act together before it's too late! God's strategy for the end-time harvest is already set in motion. Phase One is underway, and Phase Two is close behind. If you don't want to be left out tomorrow, you need to take action today. With startling insight, T.D. Jakes sets the record straight. You'll be shocked to learn how God is separating people into two distinct categories. One thing is certain—after reading The Harvest, you'll know exactly where you stand with God. This book will help you discover who will and who won't be included in the final ingathering and determine what it takes to be prepared. If you miss *The Harvest*, you'll regret it for all eternity!